RACHEL

love

from

Uncle David

Christmas

1978

THE GIFT OF A LAMB

To
Colin Smith

THE GIFT OF A LAMB

A shepherds' tale of the first Christmas
told as a verse-play by

CHARLES CAUSLEY

With music by VERA GRAY
Illustrations by Shirley Felts

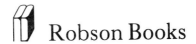
Robson Books

FIRST PUBLISHED IN GREAT BRITAIN IN
1978 BY ROBSON BOOKS LTD., 28 POLAND
STREET, LONDON W1V 3DB. COPYRIGHT ©
1978 CHARLES CAUSLEY. MUSIC
COPYRIGHT © 1978 VERA GRAY.

Causley, Charles
    The gift of a lamb.
    I. Title II. Gray, Vera
    822'.9'14   PR6005.A83G/

ISBN 0-86051-041-7

Printed in Hungary

The first performance of this play was broadcast in the BBC Radio for Schools' series *Let's Join In* on 2nd December 1977, with the following cast:

Storyteller	GARY WATSON
Ben	EDWARD KELSEY
John	LEONARD FENTON
Dan	GORDON GARDNER
Thieving Jack	CLIFFORD NORGATE
1st Angel	ROY SPENCER
2nd Angel	ERIC ALLEN
3rd Angel	ROBIN BROWNE
Joseph	HAYDN JONES
Mary	JILL SHILLING

Produced by DAVID LYTTLE

The music was played by ANNE COLLIS (percussion), SARAH FRANCIS (oboe), LIONEL BENTLEY (violin) and GEOFFREY BURFORD (piano).

CHARACTERS

Storyteller
Ben, the grandfather)
John, the son) shepherds
Dan, the grandson)
Thieving Jack
1st Angel
2nd Angel
3rd Angel
Joseph
Mary

The stage directions are given from the point of view of the actors.

(Music)

STORYTELLER: Once on a night
Both dark and chill
Three shepherds lay
Upon a hill.

Out in the black
And iron air,
Guarding their sheep
From wolf and bear.

Their watch on sheep and lamb
Ne'er ceased,
Lest they be robbed
By man or beast.

Each in a shepherd's cloak
And hood,
They lit a fire
Of winter wood.

Where grass was thin,
And thick the stones,
They tried to warm
Their bitter bones.

And quiet stars
Burned over them,
Those shepherds three
Of Bethlehem.

(Lights come up to reveal the summit of a gently-sloping hill. It is winter. On the R. slope are three shepherds: BEN, *a grizzled grandfather,* JOHN *his son, and* DAN *his grandson, all well wrapped against the cold. By them are sticks or staves, a pack of food, and one or two leather bottles. They also have, respectively, a fiddle, pipe and a drum at hand.* JOHN's *whistle-pipe is tucked in his belt. A fire glows. The dim outlines of sheep may be seen.* BEN, *leaning on a shepherd's crook, stands at the lowest level.* DAN *is seated by the fire, on which a pot of broth is being heated.* JOHN, *nearest the top of the hill, peers into the darkness watchfully.*
Music for song:

BEN:

(*sings*) I am a shepherd,
My name is Ben,
I've shepherded
Three-score years and ten.

8

Spring, summer, autumn,
Winter, too!
The years and the seasons
How they flew!
Now my nose is fire
And my hair is frost,
But never a sheep or lamb
I lost.

JOHN:

(sings) I am a shepherd,
My name is John,
I work with my father
And my son.
In forty years
Of cold and heat,
I never have lost
A lamb or sheep.
In weather gold,
In weather grey,
No sheep or lamb
Was stolen away.

DAN:	(*sings*) I am a shepherd,
	My name is Dan,
	In seven more years
	I'll be a man,
	But ever since I
	Could stand or run
	I've shepherded sheep
	In rain and sun.
	I've shepherded sheep
	On hill and moor
	As my father did,
	And his before.
BEN:	(*speaks*) Ay, that we have, a thousand seasons
	through.
JOHN:	And, if God wills, so may Dan's children too!
BEN:	Now feed the fire with sticks!
	The night is bleak.
	The sharp air pinches
	At my hand and cheek.
JOHN:	Bestir yourself, young Dan,
	And watch the pot
	That keeps the good broth
	Bubbling and hot.
BEN:	And at the stroke of twelve
	We'll sit and sup,
	And drink Dan's health
	And clink a merry cup!
	For then, my dearest grandson,
	Joy to tell,
	Comes in your birthday
	With the midnight bell!
JOHN:	Though poor we shepherds be
	And light our pay,

We have the gifts you chose
To mark the day.
To hold: a shepherd's crook,
To wear: a smock.
Then, that you choose a lamb:
First of *your* flock.

DAN: Father, grandfather, good you are and kind;
I thank you with my heart and with my mind.
And O, the lamb I choose this happy night
Is that with body black and head of white!

BEN: John, take your whistle-pipe...
(JOHN *takes it from his belt and blows a single note.*)
And Dan, your drum...
(DAN *strikes a sharp, double-tap on the drum beside him.*)

11

I, with my fiddle tucked beneath my chin...
(*He picks it up and plays a quick chord.*)
We'll play a tune,
And with a jig
Welcome Dan's birthday in.
(*They strike up. The lights fade on them.*)

STORYTELLER: But as they played
So sweet and clear,
A stranger crept
Their pasture near;
And even as
The shepherds played,
A stranger crept
From shade to shade.
He did not stand
Beneath the sky
And greet the shepherds
Eye to eye;
He did not sing,
He did not hum –
He wished no man
To hear him come,
But secretly

And without sound
He crawled across
The glimmering ground;
Over the meadow,
Up the hill,
To where the sheep and lambs
Lay still.
His brow and neck
He'd smudged with soot,
And on his face
A mask he'd put.
He carried on his back
A sack,
And the name of the man
Was
Thieving Jack.

(Lights come up on the L. slope of the hill. What at first seems to be a rock or boulder slowly begins to move. It is THIEVING JACK. *The shepherds' music is heard a little distance off, and held behind his voice as he begins to speak.)*

THIEVING JACK: Hark to the silly shepherds
As they sing and as they play –
Though what they've got to sing about
Is more than I can say.
A shepherd's lot is 'eavy,
An' a shepherd's lot is poor
In every kind o' weather you can think of –
An' some more!
They works by night an' day –
Why, it's enough to make yer weep!

If you ask me, a shepherd's
Just as silly as 'is sheep.
But that's 'is silly business,
An' as for mine, my friends,
You won't catch *me* a-workin'
All the hours the good Lord sends.
I likes to eat, I likes to drink,
I likes to lie a-bed;
I calls no man *my* master –
'Ere's what I do instead:
I nicks a little chicken
Or I bags a side o' beef,
So guard yer goods when I'm about
Because I am

a
thief!

I robs the rich AND poor –
You never
Met a worse than me:
For anything that's *yours*
Is mine,
And mine's me own,
You see.
No ducks that quack
Are safe from Jack,
Nor any sow that squealed;
Nor any sheep or lamb that's left
Unguarded in the field.
And O, but it's a lamb this night
On which I've got me eye –
I liked the black and white of it
As I went passing by.
An' so among the rocks I creep,

An' opens up me sack…
(*Very faint bleat of a lamb.*)
An' slips the lambkin in –
(*Slightly louder bleat.*)
NOW!
It belongs to Thieving Jack!
(*Bleat.* THIEVING JACK *chuckles. Bell begins to
sound midnight. Light fades L. and increases R.
SHEPHERDS play and sing on the hill.*)

BEN: (*sings*) Now the bell at midnight
       Chimes to make us glad,
       Bringing in the birthday
       Of a shepherd lad.

JOHN: (*sings*) He shall have a wooden crook,
       A smock as clean as light;
       He shall have a lambkin
       Whose wool is black and white.

(*Bell ceases striking. Light begins to grow in the sky
above the SHEPHERDS. The echo of the bell's last note
becomes a sustained, metallic sound held behind the
following:*)

DAN: *(alarmed)* Good father, and grandfather dear,
What is that light, I pray,
That burns above us in the sky
And turns the night to day?
Each spike of grass, each stone, is bright
Upon the midnight hill –
Yet lamb and sheep they soundly sleep,
And silent are, and still.

JOHN: *(gazing up, wondering)* Such fire it comes not
from the stars,
Nor comes it from the moon –
And bolder is it than the sun
That blazes at the noon.

BEN: My children, kneel;
My children, pray
That God may give us grace,
For none may know when he must go
To meet him face to face:
(Music.)
Here is a holy place.

(Music. More light. Three ANGELS *appear in the
sky above the summit of the hill. Music behind the
following:)*

16

1ST ANGEL:	Fear not, shepherds, for I bring Tidings of a new-born King – Not in castle, not in keep, Nor in tower tall and steep; Not in manor-house or hall, But a humble ox's stall.
2ND ANGEL:	Underneath a standing star And where sheep and cattle are, In a bed of straw and hay God's own Son is born this day. If to Bethlehem you go, This the truth you soon shall know.
3RD ANGEL:	And as signal and as sign, Sure as all the stars that shine,

17

	You shall find him, shepherds all,
	Swaddled in a baby-shawl;
	And the joyful news will share
	With good people everywhere.
2ND ANGEL:	Therefore, listen as we cry:
THREE ANGELS:	Glory be to God on high,
	And his gifts of love and peace
	To his people never cease.

(Light and music fade on ANGELS. *A moment of silence. The* SHEPHERDS, *bewildered, exchange glances, shake their heads, rub their eyes.)*

DAN:	Grandfather, O tell me clear,
	Did *you* see and did *you* hear
	Angel-voices, angel-gleam?
	Do I wake? Or do I dream?
BEN:	*(reassuring)* Why, indeed the angels came...
JOHN:	*(quickly)* And I heard and saw the same...
BEN:	So, with swift and fearful tread,
	Let us to that cattle-shed.
DAN:	But the night is dark and deep.
	Who will watch the lambs and sheep?
BEN:	Dearest grandson, do not fear;
	God will keep them safely here:
	Guard the hill and guard the plain
	Soundly till we come again.
	(He smiles, and removes the pot from the fire.)
JOHN:	Then let's music play...
DAN:	And sing!
BEN:	For we go to greet a King!

(Music.)

SHEPHERDS: *(sing)* High in the heaven
A gold star burns
Lighting our way
As the great world turns.

Silver the frost
It shines on the stem
As we now journey
To Bethlehem.

White is the ice
At our feet as we tread,
Pointing a path
To the manger-bed.

19

(They go off R., singing. Their voices fade. Silence.
Then, a couple of long moans from THIEVING JACK.
We see him lying in a heap on the hill-side as though
struck by a thunderbolt. The SHEPHERDS *approach*
from back L., following a winding path down the
hill. Music.)

SHEPHERDS: *(sing)* High in the heaven
A gold star burns
Lighting our way
As the great world turns...

(They break off.)
BEN: Why, mercy me, who's this I see
All white and wan and shaking...
(THIEVING JACK gives a loud groan.)
Flat on his back and with a sack –
And what a noise he's making!
(More groans.)
JOHN: Good stranger, own: was it a stone
That sent you downhill clattering?
(Groans and chattering teeth from THIEVING JACK.)
And is that why you moaning lie,
And all your teeth a-chattering?
(Groans and more chattering teeth. The SHEPHERDS
group themselves about THIEVING JACK *as he sits*
up, greatly shaken.)
THIEVING JACK: My friends, tonight was such a sight
Above me in the 'eavens,
It's blown me wits to bits – I'm all
At sixes and at sevens.
I saw the fire of fifty suns,
The sky was broken wide,
An' all the lights of God shone down –

There was nowhere to hide!
I 'eard the sound of seven seas
Upon the beatin' shore.
The strong earth shuddered at me feet.
I 'eard a mountain roar.
There was a noise of whirrin' wings
About the place I trod,
An' at the 'eart of all, it seemed,
I 'eard the voice of God.
What means that sight, what means that
   sound
I cannot speak nor say.
Shepherds, pray help me from this place
As you go on your way –
For here Jack cannot stay.

JOHN: Rise up, master, do not fret –
You shall see the morning yet!
Keep you quiet, keep you calm;
Take my hand and take my arm:
For the light that shone around,
Cast you senseless to the ground,
Was a host of angels white
Praising Heaven in the height,
Praising Heaven on the earth,
And a King and Saviour's birth –
Long, long promised...

DAN: And, they told,
In a stable, by our fold!

BEN: Come, friend, with us through the wild
To a mother, and her child:
That, among mankind, we be
First of folk God's Son to see.

THIEVING JACK: That I will, and give you thanks.
(*They help him up, and he moves stiffly.*)

Oh, me arms! And oh, me shanks!
(*Groans.*)
Bruised me body! Bent me bones
By the sticks and by the stones!
(*Groans again.*)
Gave each finger such a crack,
I can scarcely hold...
(*Suddenly remembers the theft of the lamb. He gasps out the words:*)
Me sack!
(*The* SHEPHERDS *remain quite unconscious of the reason for* THIEVING JACK's *extra uneasiness.*)

BEN: It seems that you journeyed from market,
    good stranger,
But crossing our hill is no freedom from
    danger
Of footpad and felon, or thieving attack
From villains who'd empty the pack on your
    back!

(SHEPHERDS *strike up their music, play quietly, and even foot a brief dance while allowing* THIEVING JACK *time to pull himself together and rub away his aches. As he does so, he delivers the following aside:*)

THIEVING JACK: My eye! I'd forgotten – I've 'ad such a shock –
The black and white lamb as I stole from their
    flock!

And not only that: I'm afeared and afraid
I've robbed and I've bobbed 'em what's come
    to me aid.
Me 'ead fairly whizzes, I'm in such a jam!
To own I'm a thief it's ashamed that I am.
I'll bear the sack gentle and easy and neat,
An' 'ope that there lambkin won't let out a
    bleat.
My goodness! My badness! There's never a
    doubt,
If I does a wrong, someone's bound to find
    out.
But I've learned me lesson – I've 'ad such
    a fright;
When we gets to the stable, I'll put it all right.
(He joins the others, who move off L., singing.)

·SHEPHERDS·   *(sing)* High in the heaven
                             A gold star burns
                             Lighting our way
                             As the great world turns.

                             Silver the frost
                             It shines on the stem
                             As we now journey
                             To Bethlehem.

(They are gone. Lights come up C., as in a cave under the hill. MARY *is seated, holding the Infant Jesus.* JOSEPH *stands a little to her L. Music.)*

MARY:

(sings) Sleep, King Jesus,
Your royal bed
Is made of hay
In a cattle-shed.
Sleep, King Jesus,
Do not fear,
Joseph is watching
And waiting near.

Warm in the wintry air
You lie,
The ox and the donkey
Standing by,
With summer eyes
They seem to say:

Welcome, Jesus,
On Christmas Day!

Sleep, King Jesus:
Your diamond crown
High in the sky
Where the stars look down.
Let your reign
Of love begin,
That all the world
May enter in.

(Music of the SHEPHERDS *is heard as they
approach.* JOSEPH *stands at the entrance to the stable
to greet them as they appear round the foot of the hill
from R.)*

JOSEPH: I bid you enter, shepherds, as you come
From the world's dark with fiddle, pipe
    and drum,

And nipping fingers, and white-smoking
    breath!
My name is Joseph.
Out of Nazareth
I journeyed far with gentle Mary here,
And who, this night, a son has borne so dear.
Therefore, good shepherds from the
    mountain steep,
Draw near to where the infant lies asleep
That you may tell to all, and tell it true,
The tale of wonder now made known to you.

BEN: *(shaking him by the hand)* Joseph, we thank you
    for your welcome warm
As we step in from out the weather's harm.
Angels, Archangels in the sky looked down
And bade us leave our flocks, and to the town:
And this we did with joy, and with hearts light
That Jesus Christ, God's Son, is born tonight –
And by God's grace is given human birth
To live, with sinful man, upon the earth.
So, Mary, lady, on my knees I fall
To worship him who comes to save us all.
(He kneels.)
No gift have I to bring the Heavenly King
Save my poor fiddle, and a fiddle-string.
(He plucks it.)

29

	But this, that is my comfort and my joy,
	I freely offer to the Holy Boy.
JOHN:	And I, sweet mother, as the babe I scan,
	And see God's gift to woman and to man,
	Give him my whistle-pipe.

(He kneels and offers it to MARY.*)*

Now, haste the day
As a good shepherd, *he* will pipe and play.

DAN: *(steps forward)* Jesus, I bring a greeting fair and fine,

Proud that your birth day is the same as mine.
Alas, no gift have I in either hand,
I've neither gear nor goods at my command:
Only this drum.

(He kneels.)

But with the crowing cock
I'll have a shepherd's crook, a shepherd's smock;
Yet these I will not bring, but with the light,
My dearest gift – a lambkin black and white.
This I am promised. This is to be mine –
And mine to give: and of my love, a sign.
The lamb I'll offer, for your keep and care,
On bended knee, to mark the day we share.

(THIEVING JACK is now standing on his own.)

THIEVING JACK: *(aside)* Great blocks and bricks,
Now 'ere's a fix –
An' all of me own makin'!
If truth I tell,
To prison-cell
A journey I'll be takin'!
For 'ere I am,
That little lamb
Snug in me thievin' sack...

30

(Pause. Then he comes to a decision.)
BUT
I'll be strong
An' shame the wrong,
An' dare to give it back.
This Infant King
Of whom they sing
Is merciful and good;
So, from this day,
As best I may,
I'll do things as I should!
(He clears his throat loudly and turns towards the
SHEPHERDS.*)*
Kind shepherds three, who freely gave me aid
When on the 'ill I lay, and was afraid –
Blinded by 'eaven's light, struck by its sound,
Stiff as a stone upon the quakin' ground –
Shepherds, who raised me up and spoke
    me fair,
Comforted me, an' took me in your care:
(A deep breath.)
I was no peaceful traveller on the 'ill,
For on your sheepfold I'd long gazed my fill,
And as you watched about your
    furze-fire bright
I crept, *a robber*, to your flock last night.
The lamb that's black an' white, *I'd*
    fancied too,
An' thought, "Why, Jack, that's just the one
    for you!"
An' so I popped it in the very sack
I bears, so careful-like, upon me back.
See, as I opens it…
(Faint bleat.)

The 'ead appear...
(*Louder bleat.*)
Its Jacob-coloured coat...
(*Bleat.*)
The eye, the ear.
(*Bleat.*)
And see, my cheek is red,
My shame is sore;
I vows I'll go a-thievin' nevermore,
An' give you back the lamb; though well
   I know
For this night's work to prison I should go.
This price I'll gladly pay; but one thing lack.
Humbly I beg of you – forgive old Jack.
(*He hands the lamb over to* DAN.)

DAN:	(*warmly*) That, willingly –
JOHN:	And I –
BEN:	And I as well.
	As for the stolen lamb, we'll no man tell.
DAN:	And thanks to Jack, my gift I *now* can make.

Take it, my lady, for your Son's own sake:
This trusting lamb that on my arm now lies,
As rests on yours the God-child, pure and
   wise.
(DAN *presents the lamb to* MARY.)

THIEVING JACK:	(*kneels*) Mother – a gift I'd give him if I could.
MARY:	And that you have: a heart that's turned
	to good.

Likewise, in Jesu's name, to all I say:
Receive our thanks for these your gifts today.

JOSEPH:	Thank you for whistle-pipe, and fiddle true –
	When they are played, masters, we'll think on
	you!
MARY:	And thank you for the lamb: of sin and stain .

As innocent as him who comes to reign;
And ere you rise, and ere your ways you take,
A gift, from Jesus Christ, to *you* I make.
This goodly lamb I give to you again
As sign of God's own gift from Heaven to men.
(MARY *returns the lamb to* DAN. *Faint bleat.*)
Go, tell to all the angel-story bright:
And how you saw the word made flesh
    tonight.

BEN: That we will, lady, each with joyful heart:
And wish God's family well. And so, depart.

(*Music for song.* SHEPHERDS *and* THIEVING
JACK *sing a line of each verse solo, in turn, and mime
the way in which the various instruments mentioned
are played.*)

33

SHEPHERDS AND THIEVING JACK:	*(sing)* Fiddle, play! (Zim, zim, zim) Strike the drum! (Dum, dum, dum) Blow the pipe! (Toot, toot, toot) For Christmas come! (Clap, clap, clap)
Chorus:	Merrily! Cheerily! Let the music say – Christ was born in Bethlehem, And is born today!
Verse 2:	Beat the gong! (Dong, dong, dong) Blow the horn! (Ta, ta, ta) Sound the flute! (Tee, tee, tee) For Christ is born! (Clap, clap, clap)
Chorus:	Merrily! Cheerily! Let the music say – Christ was born in Bethlehem, And is born today!
Verse 3:	Cymbals, clash! (Clash, clash, clash) Church-bells ring! (Ding, ding, ding) Play the harp!

(Ting, ting, ting)
For Christ is King!
(Clap, clap, clap)

Chorus: Merrily!
Cheerily!
Let the music say –
Christ was born in Bethlehem,
And is born today!

(They are dancing at the play's end.)

The Opening Music. This should be played by two people at one piano, and although the top part looks rather daunting it is merely octaves for most of the piece. The chords in both parts lie easily under the hands.

The Shepherds' Song and High in the Heaven (same tune)

Simply (♩= 50)

mf

I am a shep-herd, My name is Ben I've
shep-herd - ed Three score years and ten. Spring, sum-mer, au - tumn,
Win-ter too. The years and the sea-sons How they flew. Now my nose is fire
And my hair is frost, But ne - ver - a sheep or lamb I lost.

rall.

The Shepherds' Song

I am a shepherd,
My name is Ben,
I've shepherded
Three-score years and ten.
Spring, summer, autumn,
Winter, too!
The years and the seasons
How they flew!
Now my nose is fire
And my hair is frost,
But never a sheep or lamb
I lost.

I am a shepherd,
My name is Dan,
In seven more years
I'll be a man,
But ever since I
Could stand or run
I've shepherded sheep
In rain and sun.
I've shepherded sheep
On hill and moor
As my father did,
And his before.

I am a shepherd,
My name is John,
I work with my father
And my son.
In forty years
Of cold and heat,
I never have lost
A lamb or sheep.
In weather gold,
In weather grey,
No sheep or lamb
Was stolen away.

High in the Heaven

High in the heaven
A gold star burns
Lighting our way
As the great world turns.

Silver the frost
It shines on the stem
As we now journey
To Bethlehem.

White is the ice
At our feet as we tread,
Pointing a path
To the manger-bed.

The Shepherds' Jig . An oboe, recorder, flute and drum can all join in the jig, taking different phrases of the melody – the drum keeping a constant rhythmic pattern.

Now the Bell at Midnight. A glockenspiel can play the note 'C' in crotchet rhythm all the way through this song. Xylophones could also join in if the soft sticks are used.

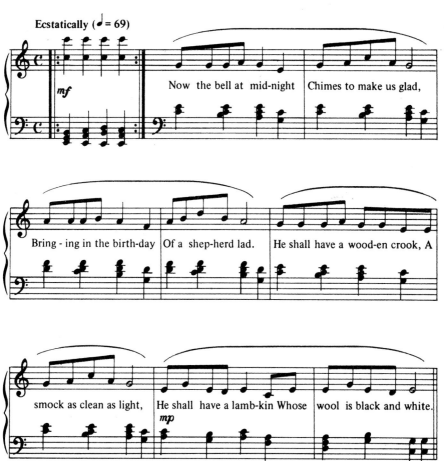

Now the bell at midnight
Chimes to make us glad,
Bringing in the birthday
Of a shepherd lad.

He shall have a wooden crook,
A smock as clean as light;
He shall have a lambkin
Whose wool is black and white.

41

The Angels' Music

SECONDO

Ethereally (♩ = 60)

pp legato

p   mp

mf

cresc.   f   ff

42

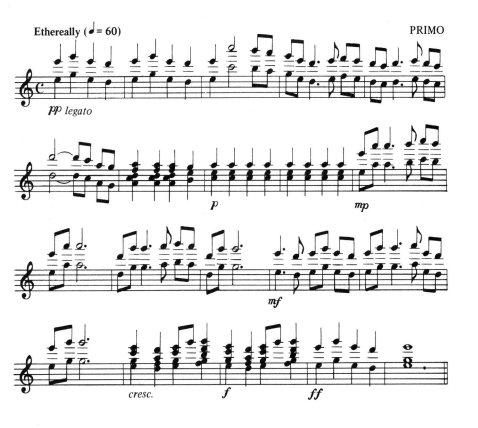

Mary's Lullaby. This song could also be used as a two-part song with the under part of the treble line being either hummed or sung to words such as 'lull-a' or 'hush-a'.

Tenderly—as a lullaby ($\downarrow \cdot = 44$)

p

Sleep King Je - sus your Roy - al bed is made of hay in a cat - tle shed. Sleep King Je - sus do not fear, Jo - seph is watch - ing and wait - ing near.

Sleep, King Jesus,
Your royal bed
Is made of hay
In a cattle-shed.
Sleep, King Jesus,
Do not fear,
Joseph is watching
And waiting near.

Warm in the wintry air
You lie,
The ox and the donkey
Standing by,
With summer eyes
They seem to say:
Welcome, Jesus,
On Christmas Day!

Sleep, King Jesus:
Your diamond crown
High in the sky
Where the stars look down.
Let your reign
Of love begin,
That all the world
May enter in.

Fiddle Play (music on opposite page). All the instruments mentioned in the verses can feature in this song. If they are pitched instruments the notes of the song can be played. The song can be sung in two parts, the voices dividing in the verses in every alternate bar.

The author suggests that the audience might learn this song before the performance in order to join in at the end.

Fiddle, play!
(Zim, zim, zim)
Strike the drum!
(Dum, dum, dum)
Blow the pipe!
(Toot, toot, toot)
For Christmas come!
(Clap, clap, clap)

Merrily!
Cheerily!
Let the music say –
Christ was born in Bethlehem,
And is born today!

Beat the gong!
(Dong, dong, dong)
Blow the horn!
(Ta, ta, ta)
Sound the flute!
(Tee, tee, tee)
For Christ is born!
(Clap, clap, clap)

Merrily!
Cheerily!
Let the music say –
Christ was born in Bethlehem,
And is born today!

Cymbals, clash!
(Clash, clash, clash)
Church-bells ring!
(Ding, ding, ding)
Play the harp!
(Ting, ting, ting)
For Christ is King!
(Clap, clap, clap)

Merrily!
Cheerily!
Let the music say –
Christ was born in Bethlehem,
And is born today!